Emily
DAVISON

WHO WAS...

Emily
DAVISON

*The girl
who gave her life
for her cause*

CLAUDIA FITZHERBERT

* SHORT BOOKS

First published in 2004 by
Short Books
15 Highbury Terrace
London N5 1UP

10 9 8 7 6 5 4 3 2 1

A CIP catalogue record for this book
is available from the British Library.

ISBN 1-904095-66-6

Printed in Great Britain by
Bookmarque Ltd, Croydon, Surrey

for my darling daughters, X & Y.

PROLOGUE

Emily Wilding Davison was an odd sort of child. She had long fair hair and a small crooked smile, and pale green eyes which darted back and forth like birds in a cage. When she was eight she went through a stage when she brought God into almost everything. God and soldiers and justice were all she talked about, for months.

"This is God's army!" she might say, after lining up her brother's toy soldiers on his bedroom floor.

"You know darling Alfred really doesn't like... "

"He needn't know."

Alfred was Emily's brother. He was three years older than her and ten times stupider. But he was the one who got to go away to school.

"Where's the justice in that?" Emily would ask.

"There isn't any, that I know of," answered Mrs Davison. "It's just the way things are."

Emily was taught at home by governesses. She was clever, anyone could see that, as greedy for books and lessons as other children were for buns and liquorice. She was reading her father's copy of *The Times* by the age of five, and by nine she had learned reams of poetry by heart, and chunks of scripture.

Her home, for the first ten years of her life, was a handsome Georgian house in warm red brick in the middle of the Essex countryside. Emily spent hours marching up and down the shrubbery outside the library, chopping the air with her long thin arms and bellowing out her favourite hymns in a mournful sing-song.

"She should have been a boy," thought her mother, watching her daughter from the nursery window. The room was full of beautiful china dolls lying neglected in their cribs. Emily had only ever wanted soldiers, little lead figures to match her brother's.

***

In the early 1880s Emily's father became involved in a

business venture in the capital, and the family moved to London. Mr Davison, afraid that his wild martinet of a daughter would miss her regular exercise in the fresh country air, taught her to skate on the round pond in Kensington Gardens and to swim in the newly built Chelsea baths. Emily took to both like an owl to the dark.

She was always either reading or rushing about, her mother complained. She never just sat, as other girls did, with some needlework in her lap and a patient look on her face.

No, agreed Emily. She hated sewing. Darling Mama. Don't be cross. You're the best mother in the world, and I'm the worst daughter. Thanks for this.

"This" was for yesterday's paper, put aside for her by her father, handed over by her mother with a sigh.

"It stretches her," said Mr Davison to his wife, when she looked doubtful about the newspaper habit. Mrs Davison's doubts remained intact. She had a frightened vision of her daughter growing as tall as the girl in the Alice picture, becoming unfit for the world.

"It's shrinking she needs, not the other," she said, gloomily.

In the newspaper Emily read reports of the debates in Parliament. She thought of the two sides in the House of Commons as opposing armies, battling it out with words. In those days the Labour party didn't exist. You were either a Liberal or a Conservative, also known as Tory. Which one was she?

"You're a Tory of course; we all are," said her mother.

Why was that?

Mrs Davison frowned. "We always have been."

It wasn't like that, said Emily. Politics wasn't fixed. It was a question of voting for whichever side you agreed with most.

"Don't look at me," said her mother, "I haven't got a vote."

Emily felt stupid. England was a democracy. Which meant rule by the people. The House of Commons was made up of the representatives of the people, put there by votes. Her mother was a person. Why didn't she have a vote?

Not everyone did.

Emily knew that. Poor people for instance, without homes to call their own. But her mother wasn't poor. So why –

She was a woman. Women didn't vote. But why?

"Oh Emily no more questions, please!" said Mrs Davison, losing patience at last. "It's just the way things are."

***

Emily was sent to France to stay with an elder half-sister on her father's side. This sister, in her thirties with a fat French husband and a babyish way of speaking, tried to teach Emily some of the tricks of the marriage trade.

"You're perfectly pwetty enough," she said. "But you mustn't wead so much. It's bad for your posture and fwightens ve fellows away."

The next thing Emily knew was that the book which she had been about to open was taken from her hands and placed on her head.

"What on earth… " Emily began. As she spoke she moved her head and the book fell into her lap. Her sister put it back: "As long as it doesn't dwop, you know you're sitting stwaight".

"I want to go home!" said Emily, with a mutinous shake of the head.

"*Oh la la*!" said the sister. "You ungwateful wwetch!"

"I want to go to school," said Emily to her parents, on the first evening of her return.

Her father, smiling, said she might as well, since she wanted it so much. But she must promise not to work too hard. They'd been a spate of articles in the paper recently, about the dangerous side-effects of study on schoolgirls.

"What sort of side-effects?" asked Emily, interested.

"Tummy aches, that sort of thing... " replied her father, vaguely.

* * *

Emily was enrolled at Kensington High, and taken there on her first morning by her father. They went together to see Miss Hitchcock, the headmistress, and Mr Davison repeated his worries about overwork.

"There's no question of that here," replied Miss Hitchcock, smiling.

She was used to fathers making a fuss. The things

men thought girls couldn't do! She blamed the mothers.

Miss Hitchcock found her new pupil an interesting case. Literature and History were Emily's passions, and they were the subjects which the headmistress took herself. In class Emily was not, as some of the other girls were, keen to show off her knowledge of a topic. She never called out an answer, nor was she the sort to stretch out an arm with a look of desperate pleading on her face. In fact she hardly bothered with answers at all, preferring to save her fire for the asking of searching questions which took her further inside a subject, further than her teacher had intended she should go. Miss Hitchcock learnt not to be surprised when in exams, more often than not, the Davison girl came top of her class.

***

Alfred, Emily's elder brother, was only ever placed at the bottom of his. "Clever clogs!" he snarled at his sister, when both their school reports came plopping through the door.

Alfred was vicious as well as stupid, always in trouble for thieving, cheating, and falling into fisticuffs with younger, weaker boys. He was a great disappointment to his father, but there was in those days a solution to the problem of problem sons: they were packed off to the Colonies, distant outposts of the Empire where young men were expected to be on the lawless side of rough. Emily was fifteen when her brother was sent away to seek his fortune in Canada, and she never saw him again. Did she miss him? Not for a second!

It was different for Mrs Davison. For years she lived for Alfred's letters, hurried little scraps of lazy nothings, which arrived at longer and longer intervals until at last they petered out altogether.

The mother's heart was broken by the silence of the son.

This made it easier for the daughter to do the things she had to do.

***

"I want to go to Holloway," said Emily, aged 19, to her parents.

"Whatever for?" answered Mrs Davison with a startled look. She was thinking of the women's prison north of the city.

Emily, laughing, explained what she meant. Holloway was the name of one of the new women's colleges attached to London University. She wanted to study for a degree in English literature.

Better a college than a prison Mrs Davison agreed, smiling. But what was the point, really, in such a course? Emily would be best off learning the arts of household management from her mother, rather than filling her head with book-learning which she was never likely to use.

Mr Davison took a different view.

"It's a good idea," he said, without saying why. The truth was that he was worried about money – clearing up Alfred's debts had more or less cleaned him out. His business venture had never prospered and for years the family had been living off a dwindling pile of capital. Now he thought: if I can scrape together the money for Emily to go to college then at least she'll be able to get a good teaching job. If it comes to that, which I hope it won't.

***

It did. Emily was only half-way through her course – and loving it, better than she'd loved anything in her life before – when her father dropped down dead without so much as a warning flicker. His widow, at a meeting with the family lawyer to see what money was left for herself and her daughter to live on, was told that there was none. She felt a fool, then, for always having supposed her husband knew best when it came to money matters. Why hadn't he told her there were problems?

Perhaps because she'd never asked.

At least they had somewhere to live. Some years earlier Mr Davison had bought a cottage in the moorland village in the north of England, where both Emily's parents had grown up. At present it was laid out as a shop, with accomodation on the first floor. The idea had always been to reconvert the shop part, back into the downstairs of the cottage, and for the couple to live there, in their old age.

Let the shop remain a shop, announced Mrs Davison, briskly. She wasn't proud, she had roots in retail, she'd always fancied a stint behind the counter.

What about me, Emily thought but did not say.

What about her daughter, Mrs Davison wondered, as she packed away her linen and counted up her china. There wasn't the money for her to stay at college, and there'd hardly be room for her at the cottage even if she wanted to come which she probably wouldn't, Mrs Davison thought, given what a darting restless creature she was and always had been. Marriage was obviously the answer except that it just as obviously wasn't. There was something about Emily, with her dangling arms and flickering eyes and the half-shy half-fervent way she had of asking questions, which marked her out as different. And if Mrs Davison knew anything at all about men it was this: they couldn't be doing with difference.

"You'd better find yourself a teaching job," she said to her daughter, at length. "Put all that learning to some use."

I should have kept her with me, Mrs Davison would think, years later, when Emily was dead. I should never have let her loose upon the world.

UNWOMANLY WOMEN

L ondon, 1906. Emily Davison tried and failed to look relaxed as she threaded her way through groups of drinkers who had spilled out onto the pavement from the public house on the corner. It was a bad time to be travelling through the city: the markets had been busy all day and now, in the unaccustomed mildness of an autumn evening, the traders were in a mood to celebrate.

"What's the hurry, darlin'?" asked one, causing the rest of his group to pause in their drinking and follow the direction of his gaze. They saw a tall, stooping woman in her early thirties with long thin arms and a small narrow head which bent beneath the piled-up weight of her braided hair. The woman's clothes – a calf-length green coat over white blouse and long grey skirt – suggested humdrum respectability; only her eyes, pale and quick and searching, hinted at a different story.

It was quieter on the other side of the street and Emily paused to take the folded piece of paper from out of her glove. She had to work out where she was, how far she had still to go. Two horse-drawn hansom carriages rumbled by, and she looked at them longingly.

If wishes were horses, she said aloud, I'd be in a hansom now.

She scanned the horizon for familiar landmarks, frowning until at last she saw the silvery tip of St George's steeple, rising like a dirty needle into the redness of the setting sun. She would be late, she realised then, and softly cursed the life which had stopped her leaving sooner.

***

She had been a governess, on and off, for ten years now. Her present situation was in a gloomy house in Kensington. Her duties were, in theory, light. She had two pupils, sisters of five and six, with whom she was expected to spend the main part of every weekday, teaching the basics of everything and the detail of nothing. From tea-time onwards she was officially free, to do as she would.

In practice, however, it was not so simple. Mrs May, her pupils' mother, was forever asking if Miss Davison would mind, very much, just popping down to the dressmaker for her, or across the park to the milliner's, to fetch some ribbon or to pay a bill. There were days, such as this one, when Emily did mind, rather a lot, but she knew better than to say so out loud. Her discontent, such as it was, ran underground.

***

The meeting, in the church basement, had been advertised to start at six. But it was nearer half past by the time Emily had found the stairs at the side of the building, and pushed open the heavy steel door. Her eyes took a moment to adjust to the dimness. When they did she saw a woman standing behind a table in the top right-hand corner of the hall, and about ten others dotted around on two benches facing the table. Emily trod carefully across the parquet floor. To see but not be seen was what she wanted most, for now.

"It was not my first time in prison," the woman behind the table was saying, "and I don't expect it to be my last. You see... "

The speaker stopped, seeing Emily. Emily also stopped, feeling like the loser in a game of grandmother's footsteps.

"Do take a seat," said the woman, in an easy, friendly voice. Emily was struck by how young she was, and how self-possessed. "All friends are welcome," the woman added, smiling.

"Oh, but I'm not... " Emily began, then fell shyly silent as some of the other women craned their necks to take a look at the disruptive newcomer.

"Are you interested in finding out more about our movement?" asked the speaker, in a clear ringing voice.

"I – yes, I think I am," said Emily.

"That makes you a friend. Please take a seat."

Emily did as she was told, and the speaker resumed her speech:

"Why do you think," she was asking now, "that the married woman has no legal right of guardianship over her children? Or the unmarried mother no claim on the father of hers? Why does the working woman earn less than her brother, and why is she forced out of the workplace as soon as she takes a husband? Why is it always the woman who is tried for the dreadful crime of leaving her baby out to die, and her partner never? I can tell you why. These are the laws which men have made to punish women. We shall never have justice until we have a say in the making of the law. That is why we women need the vote."

Emily's face, as she listened, was fierce with thought. She remembered the confusion she had felt, as a child, when she'd first discovered her mother to be voteless. "It's just the way things are," her mother had said. And the way they were still. But not the way they would be for much longer, if the will of the women behind the recent disturbances was anything to go by.

The disturbances were directed at Liberal politicians. For many years it had been assumed that the Liberal party, which had spent the last decade out of office, was the party most likely to give votes to women. It was the more progressive party, and had many individual members in favour of extending the right to vote to their wives and sisters, not to mention their mothers. But earlier that year the Liberals had been swept to power without actually promising votes for women, and the subject had been ignored by the government in the months which followed.

This had made a few women very angry indeed – for so long they had waited patiently for a reforming government, and this was their reward! Several had been arrested after disrupting political speeches with their demand for "the vote this session". The newspapers were full of stories about these "unwomanly women" – the *Daily Mail* came up with the name "suffragette" for them. Emily had come along to the meeting partly out of curiosity.

"Any questions?" the speaker was asking now, scanning the room with bright green eyes set like saucers in her wide-open face.

Emily felt a hotness. She knew she was expected to say something. She was the newcomer, after all.

"I wonder... " she began, "I mean, it seems to me... what I'm trying to say is that violence is never justified, surely?"

There was a murmur from the benches just in front,

with one woman saying, in a prim voice – "Don't look at us dear."

"Well," Emily stammered. "Maybe not you... but those two who were arrested in the beginning, I heard – or rather read – that they were very rough."

Low laughter from the audience and then the speaker held up her hand.

"Do I look rough to you?" she said.

"No... no!" said Emily, much too shy to stare.

The speaker then introduced herself as Christabel Pankhurst, one of the two who had been arrested in the beginning.

"I'm sorry," said Emily, "I didn't... "

"No," agreed Christabel, smiling. "How could you?"

***

Christabel meant to intrigue Emily, and she succeeded. While the other women dispersed, mumbling promises about the next meeting, the governess lingered shyly, hoping to find out more. "Would you like to walk back to the office with me?" Christabel asked, as she gathered up the pamphlets displayed on the table. "It isn't far."

Emily wondered what it was about Christabel that had made her question seem like a command. Charisma, she decided, was the answer. Christabel had a power over people. It was called charisma.

The office turned out to be quite far after all. About an hour's walk altogether, with Christabel talking non-stop all the way. Talking fast and walking even faster. Emily strode to keep up, her ears flapping, her heart pounding. Christabel had a thrilling way of looking at the world. She turned everything upside down, history, politics, the law, science, in her search for pointers to a brave new future. Then she talked about her father, a lawyer who had stood up for underdogs all his life before dying of overwork while still in his prime.

"And your mother? Is she also... dead?" asked Emily.

Christabel laughed and said that her mother was probably the least dead woman in the whole of England. It was she who had started up the new campaign, she added, not that there was anything new about her belief in the cause of women's suffrage.

"So what would you say was new about this

campaign, exactly?" asked Emily, wishing she knew the subject better.

"It's a question of having run out of patience," Christabel explained, patiently. "Mother says the difference between our organisation – the Women's Social and Political Union – and any that have gone before is that members of the Union are prepared to sacrifice life itself for the vote."

"Is that… true… do you think?"

Christabel's glance was sharp. "It's true of Mother. Where she leads, others will follow."

Emily thought about her own mother, shrunk and loving and anxious, rocking in her chair in her cottage on the moor. She looked away from the thought, feeling guilty. Old Mrs Davison was owed a visit.

"Do you have a degree?" Christabel asked her then. Emily explained about having to leave Holloway early, after her father's death, and earn her living as a governess.

"But I carried on studying" she said, not without pride. "In the evenings. I got a First actually."

"Join the club," said Christabel, smiling. "Mine's in Law. But of course there is no question of a woman being allowed to practise as a lawyer. God forbid!"

Emily nodded in sympathy. She would never have gone in for teaching, she sometimes thought, if she'd been able to support herself any other way. But what else was there? Recent inventions – first of the typewriter and then of the telephone – had led to an explosion of clerical jobs. But they did not pay a living wage to women who had to sort out their own board and lodging.

Emily had a theory about the reasons for this: for centuries it had been supposed that women's brains were weaker than men's, less suited to hard mental work. And now that women were beginning to go to university, and proving that they were quite as clever, if not cleverer, than their brothers, the men had grown afraid of being swamped by women, and were determined to keep them out for that reason.

True, mused Emily, the medical profession had been forced, some years earlier, to allow women to train as doctors, but that had taken great persistence on the part of the few pioneers who had received their own training abroad before setting up a medical school for women in London. Perhaps something similar could be achieved by women wanting to be lawyers?

"Did you ever think of refusing to take no for an answer?"

"Oh yes!" said Christabel, smiling, "In fact I went some way down that path. But then I decided my energies could be better spent. You see, for years women have divided their energies between different campaigns. Some have worked to change the marriage laws, others for better education, some for the right to train for specific professions, others for right to vote. But really it is the last which counts, before all the others. If we had the vote we could work for improvements from *inside* the system, rather than always knocking on the door with our begging bowls. People say, about the vote, be patient, it will happen. I reply, it will only happen because a generation of women will rise up to make it happen. We are that generation, Miss Davison. Our time has come."

When at last they reached the office – which was in a building called Clement's Inn – Emily looked at her watch and said she'd better be going; she was expected back at the house.

"Come upstairs first," said Christabel. "Meet Mother."

Emily needed no further persuasion. She followed Christabel up a clattering stone staircase into a large light room on the fourth floor. Emily looked around with interest. There were three desks in the room, piled high with paperwork, a sofa with some beautiful brightly patterned cloth thrown over it, any old how, and a miniature grate from which a small coal fire threw out fitful flames. The sloping walls were painted in peeling green and the dull red carpet didn't quite reach the edge of the wooden floor. The whole effect was oddly cosy. Perhaps because of the tiny elegant woman sitting at a tea tray under the window, pouring from silver into flowered porcelain.

"Darling!" she said, her face lighting up at the sight of Christabel. "Are you exhausted?"

"Christabel is never exhausted," said a tinkling voice from behind the desk in the furthest corner of the room. Emily looked across at a woman who looked like a poodle, except that her nose was red instead of black.

"I'm Mrs Tuke," said the poodle, smiling at Emily,

29

"secretary and general dogsbody."

"And this is my mother," said Christabel casually, flopping down on the comfortable-looking sofa.

"Are you… ? Is she… ?" Mrs Pankhurst turned an elegant face of delicately raised eyebrows first to Emily, then back to Christabel.

"Oh she's one of us alright," said Christabel, and as she spoke she looked at Emily in a way which made Emily feel caressed all over. Caressed and cornered. For the truth was that she wasn't one of them. Not yet anyway. But she didn't feel like saying so, somehow.

"She's a bit worried about the violence," added Christabel, lingering on the word.

Mrs Pankhurst stood up, and came to take one of Emily's hands in her own. "The violence," she said, fixing Emily with a beseeching stare from the violet pools of her eyes, "has to be seen to be believed."

Emily was at once transfixed and embarrassed. The poodle-woman, meanwhile, after rummaging about on her desk had come up with a flyer containing details of further events and meetings.

The governess took the paper, gratefully, and said her goodbyes.

DOUBLE LIFE

The next suffragette meeting which Emily attended was a much larger affair altogether. Several hundred women had gathered together in a rented hall close to the Houses of Parliament. The plan was for Mrs Pankhurst to lead the first group of about twenty women to the House of Commons, where she would ask to see the Prime Minister, and then for groups of a similar size to come up behind her.

"He won't agree to see us," explained Mrs Pankhurst, "and we must simply refuse to be moved along. They will try not to arrest us for the very reason that we want to be arrested. Arrest is newsworthy. News is advertisement. The government knows this.

That is why they try to ignore our protests. They don't want the spectacle of respectable women being tried for breaches of the peace. But if we refuse to be pushed back then in the end the police will have no choice. The government must do us justice or do us violence."

Emily stood at the back, missing nothing. Christabel had said of her mother's voice that it was her "unsecret weapon" and no wonder. The tone was low and mournful and yet it carried, without apparent effort, to the farthest reaches of the hall where Emily was standing.

The governess trailed behind one of the groups as they made their way to the Strangers' Entrance of the House of Commons. "I'm only here to watch" she had told herself. "I won't get involved."

But then she found she couldn't not get involved. Not when she saw the orderly procession of marchers being broken up by mounted policemen who charged the women this way and that, scattering them like leaves.

"Why don't you just let them through?" she asked one of the more approachable-looking, unmounted policemen, when she reached the front of a surging crowd in which suffragettes, spectators and rowdies were all mixed up.

"Why don't you just mind your own business?" the policeman snarled back, and Emily felt the hatred in his voice like a slap on the face. She moved away, keeping her eyes fixed on a new group of women who were trying to push through the cordon of police which guarded the entrance to the Commons.

This was the sort of behaviour which had shocked Emily, when she had first read about it in the newspaper. In print it had sounded so rough and childish, this physical resistance to the forces of law and order. But now she saw how it was – the women asked only to be received or to be arrested. It was the police – acting on orders no doubt – who prolonged the physical battle by resisting the women, manhandling them often, but delaying arrest for as long as possible. Arrest was a mercy which the suffragettes had to earn by refusing to melt away. To think that all this horror could be avoided by the Prime Minister simply agreeing to see the women made Emily's blood boil.

She had decided to try and work her way back

through the crowd and join the next batch of marchers when she saw a policeman raise his fist to one of the women just in front of her in the crowd, and knock her down to the ground. At once she tried to go to the woman, to see if she was alright but the people kept pressing in around her, blocking her view. Then she saw a sturdy-looking man stop and stoop and she relaxed. The woman would be alright now – the man would get her out of the scrum... But what had that policeman been thinking of?

Never mind the policeman – what was the man up to? He'd stood up from stooping and now he was – no, he couldn't be – yes, he was.

"Get off her!" Emily had reached the man and was trying to pull him away. He turned round, with a surprised look on his face which fast congealed to fury.

"Get off me!" he growled, pushing Emily sideways onto the ground before disppearing into the crowd.

"Are you alright?" it was the woman whose rescue she had come to in the first place, smiling down at her. She was only a girl, Emily saw now, nineteen or twenty at the most, with eyes which danced merrily over the bloody mess of her lips and nose.

"I suppose so," said Emily. "Who was he?"

"Just a hooligan having fun," the girl replied. As she spoke she put a hand in the side where the man had kicked and winced at the pain.

"I'm Emily."

"Mary," said the girl, thrusting a gloved hand into Emily's and helping her up. "Mary Leigh. Are you one of us?"

Emily hesitated. She was resolved to become one, but did something have to happen first?

Mary, reading her face, smiled and said: "I think you've just had your first suffragette experience."

***

The governess knew better than to tell her employers of her new and urgent interests. She didn't lie to them, exactly – just neglected to mention the truth. At first it was merely a question of keeping her reading matter secret. Then Spring came, and the governess's double life took an outdoor turn.

"Good stroll?" Mrs May would ask, when Emily came in of an evening.

"Yes thank you," Emily would answer, and go on to describe where she had been without telling the full story. So, for instance, she might say – " I watched the sunset in the park," and not explain that her vantage point had been the back of a trailer, from where she had made a speech to passers-by about the government's wickedness in ignoring women's claim to citizenship. Or she would enthuse about the view from the top of a nearby hill, but not explain about the pavements she had chalked on the way there, with details of suffragette meetings and events.

Why didn't Mrs May guess that something was afoot? Too distracted, probably, by her husband's moods.

Mr May was a small, foxy man with clear, cold eyes and a high, squeaky voice. Emily only ever saw him at the breakfast table, where he sat behind the newspaper, and barked about the world "going to the dogs". The motor car was a favourite object of ridicule – he called it the "modern cart" (ha ha) – with the suffragettes coming a close second.

"They're becoming more of a menace than a joke," he might say.

Or: "They're everywhere, damned women! Absolutely everywhere!" and as he spoke he would shake the newspaper as though to make sure that there weren't any minxes lurking in the centre pages.

And Emily, smiling, would think that her friends were doing very well.

***

And so they were. Between 1906 and 1908 the suffragettes opposed the government at by-elections, interrupted speeches by politicians, chained themselves to the railings outside Downing Street to advertise the Cause and shouted through a megaphone at members of parliament from a cruiser on the Thames. There was also a series of processions and marches, organised riots of purple, white and green – these were the official colours of the Union, used to great effect on banners held aloft over the crowd, which were designed to advertise the sheer numbers of women who desired the vote.

The Prime Minister, Mr Asquith, remained unmoved. It was not just a question of what women wanted, he argued, but of what they ought to want. It was a woman's job to offer a chap some rest from the wear and tear of politics. Mrs Pankhurst and her followers were simply a posse of lunatic, unsexed creatures who had lost their way. These thoughts and others the Prime Minister would fire off in daily letters to a young woman called Venetia with whom he was besotted. She didn't bother him about votes, thank God. "Pretty girls have better things to think about than women's rights," he sometimes said, with a stupid smile.

In the summer of 1908, the Prime Minister's wife was arranging flowers in the upstairs drawing room, humming an aria from the opera which she had attended the night before, when she was rudely interrupted by the sound of splintering glass. She watched aghast as a pane of the window fell inwards, then bent to pick up the stone which had done the damage. It was wrapped in a piece of paper, on which was written, in a large, rounded hand: "Votes for Women".

"Are you hurt, Ma'am?" asked a servant, rushing in. No, she said, she wasn't.

"But that's not the point, really, is it? The point is that I might have been," is what she would say in the future, with a delicate yawn, whenever the subject of women's suffrage is mentioned. The Prime Minister's wife was no more bothered about votes than young

Venetia. Both had power enough without.

**

The window-smashing marked a new stage in the militant suffrage campaign. The publicity was tremendous, with the papers unanimous in their contempt.

"What exactly is a suffragette, Papa?" asked the youngest of Mr May's daughters one morning, as she squinted at her father's newspaper, upside down.

Emily felt herself stiffen. Barks were one thing. Conversation quite another. Would she, could she, should she now come clean?

The Head of the Family smelt her fear.

"Ask your governess, why don't you!" he said to the child, before picking up a spoon and hitting his egg with a violence which sent the top spinning across the table.

"A suffragette is a woman who… " Emily began, feeling the red rising.

"A suffragette is NOT a woman!" the Head of the Family interrupted her, banging the table hard.

"A suffragette is a hyena!"

Emily knew then that she must declare her hand.

"I am a believer... " she said, standing up and

throwing her napkin on the table, "...in the Cause!"

"What does she mean?" asked Mrs May, flustered and fretful.

"She means she's a paid-up member of the suffragette movement, damn it all!" replied her husband, his red fox-face white with anger.

"Conviction costs nothing!" said Emily, sweetly, before leaving the room. She didn't mean to lie.

Mrs May came to see her in the schoolroom a few hours later.

"I expect you want me to leave," said Emily, sounding harsher than she felt.

"Oh no... it's just that... my husband does ask that you put aside these... these... foolish notions about votes for women. I know in some ways it doesn't matter, much, what you think. You're only the governess after all. But we're afraid you might inadvertently infect the children with your views... "

Emily cocked her head. She didn't want to be rude. Best say nothing then, she thought.

"You're quite wrong, you know, to think women having a say will make the country a better place."

No comment.

"Women have... erm... other duties. We can't get involved in politics. We haven't got the time."

This was a bit rich coming from Mrs May who did absolutely nothing with her time. Never had, never would. As she very well knew. In fact, the last thing Mrs May wanted to do was to have to find another governess. Throwing pride to the wastepaper basket, she made a last ditch attempt to keep the one she had.

"Perhaps if you would just agree to *pretend* not to believe?"

But Emily had had a sniff of life on the other side.

"No." she said. "No; it's best that I go. I need to be free."

"What for?" asked Mrs May exasperated.

"Free to go to prison," replied the governess with a happy, crooked smile.

***

Emily, counting up her savings, found she had enough to support herself for about a year, if she was very careful. She was not sorry to leave the Mays. In fact she felt light-headed with relief at having taken a step into the unknown. Light-headed and reconnected to a younger, more hopeful version of herself. For years she had been pretending, in public, to a cheerfulness she did not feel about the narrow confines of her life. "Is this all there is, then, to my time on earth?" was the question which had begun to haunt her.

Meeting Christabel had changed everything. The younger woman's confident assumption that she had been put into the world in order to transform it had deeply impressed the governess, as had her argument that women had better work for the vote before anything else. Emily felt as though she had been given, on a plate, both a reason for living and a way of life. From now on she would, quite simply, live for the Cause. She would not worry about money until money worried her.

DANGER WORK

Within a week of leaving her governessing post, Emily had taken a room, plain but clean, in a respectable-seeming lodging house not far from Clement's Inn.

"Will you be in much, miss, during the day like?" asked the landlady.

"Oh no, I shouldn't think so. You see I'm going to devote myself to… "

Emily faltered, seeing the narrowly inquisitive look in the other woman's eyes. There would be time enough to tell the landlady how she spent her days. For the moment she merely paused then said: "…voluntary work. I'm going to devote myself to voluntary work."

"Indeed," said the landlady with a faint raising of

pencilled brows. "Well it's breakfast at eight and no gentleman callers after five. That suit you?"

"Oh yes. Thank you" said Emily, with a rueful smile at the gentleman rule. She was surprised it wasn't obvious that she had other fish to fry.

She called at Clement's Inn as soon as she was settled.

"It's Miss Davison isn't it?" said Mrs Tuke.

"Yes," said Emily, taken aback at the asking of the question. Surely they knew who she was by now? She'd been coming to the weekly meetings for nearly three years.

"You mustn't think we don't know you," said Christabel, reading her mind. "It's just the name business. We have so many."

Of course they did. At once Emily felt ashamed that she had even thought of taking offence. What, after all, had she ever done for the movement, that she should be remembered above the hundreds of others who came by the office?

"I've come to tell you that my circumstances have changed," she said, in an embarrassed rush. "I've left my situation and am available... for 'danger work'."

It was a phrase she had heard on Christabel's lips some months earlier. At one of the weekly At Home meetings women available for danger work had been asked to stay behind after the rest had gone. Emily had longed to be of their number. Now she was.

Christabel smiled at her warmly. "You are ready for… prison?" she asked, gently.

Emily nodded.

"And the hunger strike?"

"Oh yes. That too."

The suffragette hunger strike had been started the previous month by one of the rank and file and was being vigorously supported by the Pankhurst leadership. The idea was for the prisoners to refuse to eat anything at all in a bid to improve their prison conditions. The tactic, so far, had worked a treat: several hunger-striking women had been released early from their sentences. The last thing the government wanted was a death on their hands.

"Well," said Christabel. "You should know our methods well enough by now. Find a meeting and plan your protest. I look forward to reading about it."

***

Emily arranged to go with her friend Mary Leigh to Limehouse, in the East End of London, where the Chancellor of the Exchequer was due to make a speech about the new taxes in the Budget. The Chancellor himself was known to be in favour of votes for women but that made no difference to suffragette tactics: he was a member of a government which refused to help the women, and for that reason his speeches would be interrupted.

But making an interruption was no longer as easy as it had once been. The Liberals had responded to suffragette tactics by banning all women from political meetings. The suffragettes had responded by leaning on their brothers and husbands, and the result was that there was now a small network of men prepared to start the ball rolling, on the interruption front.

***

"Gentlemen," said the Chancellor, putting away his notes.

It was stuffy in the hall and the windows were open, letting in the sounds of the street, the occasional dying fall of a stall-holder's cry. But the noise from without was nothing compared to that rising up from inside the hall – a rolling surge of rustling and shuf-fling which threatened to drown the Speaker before his speech was even begun.

"Gentlemen!" he said again, louder and crosser than before. "Gentlemen –"

"And where's the ladies is what we'd like to know!" shouted a male voice from the middle row.

"Shame on you for shutting them out!" joined in another.

"Call yerselves Liberals, it's a bleedin' disgrace!"

The stewards sprang into action, walking along the rows of men until they reached the pockets of protes-tors. There was only a handful altogether. A handful was all it ever took.

Emily Davison sat still as a bird in one of the tall houses which backed onto the hall. She was perched by the window in a room on the second floor, with a megaphone dangling from her hand. Mary Leigh, standing sentry at the other window, was holding another just the same.

It was Mary who'd known which tram to catch and where to change and what to do when once they were on their feet again. "Hold your nose and follow me," she had said to Emily as she led the older woman through a maze of little alleys.

"I used to live here," she added, as they came out of a fetid tunnel into a long avenue of tall, thin houses.

Emily, looking around, thought about how little she knew of Mary's life outside the Movement. Then she corrected the thought with another: Mary's life, like her own, was the Movement. It was more a question of knowing nothing of what had gone before.

They'd been let into the house and ushered upstairs by a kindly-looking man dressed in a tattered vest and trousers. Mary began to introduce herself, but the man cut her short. "I know as much as I need to know," he'd said, and ushered them upstairs.

***

In the hall, the men who'd caused the commotion were taken away by the stewards and handed over to the police, who had been loitering with intent in the street outside.

Emily and Mary craned their necks to see what happened next. Nothing. No arrests.

"Just as well," said Mary, smiling. Male supporters

had their uses, to be sure, but it would muddle the picture for the prisons to start filling with men as well as women.

"Are you ready?" Mary asked Emily and Emily nodded. She was waiting for her cue. It came to her faintly, shortly after the Chancellor resumed his speech.

"Gentlemen, let me tell you this, the People's Budget… "

Emily looked at Mary and saw her friend's thumb held high in the air. Time to act. She knelt on the floor, lent as far as she dared out of the window, put the megaphone to her lips and shouted: "Aren't women people too?"

The police on duty in the street below looked up and around. It wasn't hard to spot the angular woman with the flyaway hair sticking halfway out of the window with a megaphone in her hand.

"Stop that!" cried one. Emily, smiling, began again: "Aren't women people too? When will the government give votes to women?"

The police conferred, and then four of them set off together down the street. They disappeared from sight as they turned into the avenue of tall thin houses which backed onto the hall where the meeting was taking place.

"They'll be a good five minutes yet," says Mary, and lent out of her own window, megaphone at the ready.

"Votes before taxes! Votes for women! DEEDS NOT WORDS!" The slogans fell like drops of rain on the unprotected heads of passers-by gathered in the street below. Some smiled and others scowled: it was a question less of mood than of minds already made up.

The old man in the vest stood to one side as the policemen piled into the house. He didn't try to detain them. He rather thought he'd done his bit.

Emily, hearing the pound of police feet on the stairs, smiled at Mary. Everything had gone according to plan.

"Come along now you two. You know you can't do that here. Down to the station with you."

"Arrested for asking questions! Gentlemen consider the justice please of arresting women for asking questions!" shouted Emily into her speaker, out of the window, as the coppers closed in.

***

Emily and Mary spent the night in police custody and were taken to court the following morning. The Magistrate, seeming half-asleep behind his half-moon glasses, didn't take long to hear their cases.

"Two months," he murmured, when Emily was in the dock. "Unless," he added, with an absent-minded pick of the ear, "the accused would prefer to pay a fine?"

The suffragettes didn't believe in paying fines instead of serving time.

"Over my dead body," answered Emily, with a bold tilt of her squarish chin.

"And I thought it was just a way of talking," the Magistrate would say to his wife some years later, when Emily's picture was in all the papers. He wasn't a man to forget a face. The half-asleep look was just a mask.

**

Emily and Mary were taken together in a horse-drawn prison van to Holloway Gaol in north London. It was a prison for women only, designed and run by men. "I only work here," said the wardress who met them at the gate. "Don't take your protest out on me."

The prisoners were led under a red brick arch to the new wing of the old stone prison. They were shown into a changing area which reeked of disinfectant, and each of them was issued with a pile of prison clothes. Then the wardress turned her back, to attend to other business. Emily, seeing her chance, changed quickly and managed to transfer a small hammer from the pocket of her coat to the lining of her baggy regulation knickers.

The prison clothes were hideous: patched and stained underwear, scratchy green serge dress patterned with regulation arrows and ill-fitting unmatching shoes which could have been out of the Iron Age they weighed so much. But Emily had never minded much about clothes and wasn't going to start now.

The cell was another matter: Emily was horrified by the small dark box in which she would be expected to spend most of her days in solitary confinement. The floor and walls were made of clammy concrete, and the only furniture was a plank bed, low on the ground, a hard little stool and a table attached to the wall. The cell was clean, on account of how new it was, but unpleasantly airless. There was one small window, set high in the wall, which Emily could reach, just, by standing on the stool.

Which is what she did, as soon as she was left alone – it was the work of a moment to smash the single pane.

"It's my ventilation protest," explained Emily, in her most governessy voice, to the wardress who came running.

"What the… " began the wardress. Then she saw the little hammer among the shards of broken glass glinting on the concrete floor. Her fault for not checking. Nothing more was said.

"I won't be eating," said Emily civilly, as she was frog-marched to another cell.

"I daresay not," replied the wardress, locking her in.

There were several suffragettes in cells on the same floor but they were not allowed to see or speak to one another. It made no difference: the hunger strike spread like wildfire. It was part of their protest, they explained to the Governor. They would starve for as long as they were kept in solitary.

The Governor was as reasonable as his indifference

allowed. He told the women that they had to be kept apart because they made such a racket when they were together.

"We need to sing songs to keep our spirits up," replied the suffragettes. We're political prisoners, they added, not common criminals.

Could have fooled us, said the prison officials, replacing the lunch trays with the supper, sniffing at the untouched food.

The other prisoners, many of whom were doing time for selling sex to feed their children, looked on amazed. Most belonged to the starving end of poor. Prison food, as far as they were concerned, was the silver lining of prison life.

Emily was released early from her two-month sentence after five days without food. Six other hunger strikers were freed the same day. At the prison gates they were met by a welcoming committee, headed by Mrs Tuke, and taken to a celebration breakfast at a London hotel.

Emily ate a kipper and felt sick. Mrs Tuke saw her leave the table and followed her into the Ladies.

"Have you anywhere to go?" she asked kindly,

frowning as Emily retched into the sink. "You may need looking after."

Emily thought about the loneliness of her rented room, and the landlady who had failed to become a friend.

"I've got Mother," she said, with a sad, brave smile.

**

Mrs Davison was distraught. For years she had minded her own and other people's business, behind the counter of her cake-shop. It was known, roundabout, that she had a clever daughter with a university degree and a teaching career who made occasional visits home. But now that daughter had become a jailbird – there'd been a piece about her in the local paper – and Mrs Davison could not bear to meet the greedy, sympathetic glances of her neighbours when they came to buy their cakes.

She tried to make Emily understand what she minded, and why.

"All the neighbours are talking about you," she began, after sitting her daughter in front of the fire and taking a brush to the tangles in her long, fair hair.

"That's good," says Emily. "It's one of the reasons for doing the things we do. To make people think."

"Talking isn't thinking."

"No but–"

"And thinking isn't approving."

"No, Mother, I agree. But on the other hand–"

"There is no other hand, Emily. They regard you as a dangerous freak!"

"Mother please. Don't get upset. I'm sorry… "

"Stop then."

"Mother!"

"Show me you're sorry by stopping. If you can't stop then you're not sorry."

"I am sorry… I'm sorry for upsetting you."

"Then promise."

"I can't do that Mother. Not even for you. If only you would let me explain some things about the movement… "

"No."

"But… "

"I won't hear about it. To me it's wrong. Which isn't to say I believe or disbelieve in votes for men or women, cats or dogs," she added, holding the brush

56

aloft. "That's just politics and all politics is nonsense but there's no harm in it I suppose as long as you're peaceful."

"In that case why…?"

"As long as you're peaceful Emily! It's the going to prison I can't be doing with. If only… "

Mrs Davison stopped talking and looked away, to hide from her daughter the sight of the fat, frustrated tears rolling down her cheeks.

But Emily was blind both to the tears and the clumsy attempt to hide them. She was leafing through a book about political protest, searching for the sentence which would, she said to her mother, "explain everything".

"Please!" said Mrs Davison, "Please! We agreed… "

"Here it is!" interrupted Emily, pink in the face with the pleasure of finding:

"*Under a government which imprisons any unjustly, the true place for a just man – or woman – is also a prison.*"

There's nothing unjust about locking you up, her mother thought, but did not say.

STROKED WITH A SAW

By the end of September 1909, Emily Davison had served three prison sentences and had become an old hand at hunger-striking her way to freedom. She was one of several hundred women who were making a laughing stock of the government. What was the point of putting the women away if they couldn't keep them there?

"Let them die!" argued the angrier of the anti-suffragists, in the papers and in parliament. But the government didn't dare. The Ministers were afraid of a suffragette death, afraid of what it might do for the Cause. But nor were they happy to let the early releases continue. The Prime Minister, Mr Asquith, new to the job and bored of the Cause, made a decision.

Quietly, without warning or discussion, he authorised the Home Secretary to allow the prison governors to take action against the hunger-striking women.

"Hospital treatment" was the cosy name given to the process used. Everyone knew it was anything but.

***

Mary Leigh, in prison in Birmingham for disrupting a meeting there, was one of the first victims of the new regime. Emily went to see her when she was released, and was shaken by the state of her.

"Was it as bad as…" Emily hesitated, searching for the most unpleasant experience she could think of.

"Worse," croaked Mary. And then she tried to warn Emily what to expect, if she decided to serve another term in jail.

But Emily no longer felt she had any choice in the matter. After leaving her last job she had committed herself to the Cause with the full force of her passionate nature. She understood better now why she had taken so long to volunteer for danger work. It was as though she had known, without knowing that she knew, that the rest of life would fall away, as soon as she embarked on militancy proper. Now, when she looked back on her past enthusiasms – for swimming, music, the theatre, old friendships – she saw them as the props and struts of a building which stood empty and unused.

"Of course I'll be going again," she said to Mary.

"Better make a Will first, then," said her friend, only half in jest.

***

"I am going to have to feed you by force."

Emily shivered, and shrank deeper into her prison cell. It was November now and she thought she had never been so cold in her life before. Her own fault for not bringing warmer clothes. (It had become part of the suffragettes' protest, to refuse to wear prison uniform, and the authorities seemed unwilling to force the issue.)

"This is your last chance Davison. If this food remains untouched on my return I shall feed you by force."

The doctor was speaking through a keyhole at mouth level. Emily heard him walk away and then she heard the warden turn a key. The food flap was opened and a tray pushed onto a shelf on the inside of the cell door. Then the flap was pulled shut.

Emily determined not even to look and see what was on offer. Succulent smells filled the dank dark cell. She guessed roast chicken, with crispy potatoes and some buttery veg. The prison food had improved beyond all recognition since the hunger strike began. Or was it just that bad food smelt good when you were starving? Emily thought not. She had heard other women speak, often enough, about the chunks of black bread served butterless and jamless during their first spells inside. The porridge which looked and tasted like glue. The gristle served up as meat floating in grease served up as gravy.

When the hunger strike began it was little hardship turning that muck down. And once the hunger strike had started there was no turning back. That was what the authorities failed to understand, silly old fools. These women weren't for turning.

**

Emily thought she knew what to expect when the doctor came back down the corridor with his team of helpers and his feeding trolley. Mary had tried to warn her, after all. Only later did she understand that this wasn't an experience you could prepare for.

The door swung slowly open on squealing hinges. First through was the Matron, dragging the trolley behind. Then the wardresses, young women all three with heavy keys clanking at belted waists, and last of all the Doctor, a small, dapper man with waxed moustaches and wintry, pale-blue eyes. The tiny cell, bare of furniture except for the bed, felt full to bursting. Emily, breathing deeply, pushed herself against the wall, preparing to refuse to do whatever she was asked. Her palms were damp with dread.

The doctor began by asking questions.

"Can you confirm your name?"

"Votes for women."

"Religion?"

"Votes for women."

"Date of birth?"

"Votes for women."

"I cannot tell you how tedious this is for me," said the Doctor. "How many days have you been without food?"

"Votes for women."

"Very well," said the Doctor. "You have made clear

your refusal to cooperate. I shall proceed to feed you by force. Matron!"

"On the bed!" shouted Matron, a hard-faced woman with sunken eyes. Emily stood as still as the trembling allowed.

"Come along now," said the doctor in a conciliatory voice. But there was nothing conciliatory in the clasp of the hands which took Emily by the wrists. Two wardresses, one on either side, yanked her forward to the bed where they pushed her down. She shot up as soon as they loosened their grip but they were on top of her at once, forcing her back. The third wardress then took up position at the foot of the bed, holding down the prisoner's feet, while the matron stood at the head and put rough, uncaressing hands around her face.

"The more you resist the harder this will be," said the Doctor, looking down at his victim. Emily stared back with eyes she couldn't stop from being beseeching. The Doctor, twisting one end of his twirling black moustaches, let out an impatient sigh. Matron had a steel gag in one hand and the fingers of the other in Emily's mouth.

Emily tried to shake her off, but with both arms pinned down she hadn't the strength in her neck. She resolved to try and take a bite out of Matron's hand but she was no match for the grim expertise of her gaolors: just when she'd widened her jaws for the kill, Matron jammed the steel gag into place, knocking a tooth sideways.

There was a taste of blood which Emily tried to reach with her tongue but the gag was in the way. She opened her mouth to speak but the only sounds which came out were muffled and shapeless. With terrified eyes she followed the Doctor's movements as he fiddled around with the trolley.

"Here we go... " he said at last, waving some rubber tubing in the air, as though he were a conjuror and it the stuff of his next trick. Emily felt the awkward weight of him as he leant across, reaching to put the tube down her throat.

She closed her eyes and tried and failed to fix her mind somewhere else. The thickness of the tube was unbearable! They'd made a mistake she was sure. It was of a size which couldn't, *wouldn't* go down her throat without killing her. She opened eyes to tell them so but couldn't catch any of theirs before she began to choke. Well that was that, then, she thought, they would have to stop now wouldn't they? No, apparently not. She carried on feeling as though she was choking while the Doctor frowned and carried on pushing and the steel toes of the foot of the frowning Matron went tap, tap, tap on the concrete floor.

The tapping stopped when the feeding started. At a nod from the Doctor, Matron picked up a jug from the trolley and began to pour some thick brown liquid into a funnel at the other end of the rubber tube. There was a stench of old broth and medicine mixed.

"I am going to be sick," thought Emily, and promptly was. Her legs doubled up in a spasm of sickness and pain.

"Concentrate!" barked Matron to the foot-duty wardress, a slip of a thing, a secret sympathiser who would have liked nothing better than to hand in her notice then and there.

Only she couldn't. She wouldn't. She didn't dare: there was her sick old mother to think of, and her father coughing his way to an early grave. The few shillings she brought home from the prison each week were all that kept the family from starving.

Emily saw another dollop of gloop poured into the funnel and felt the nausea rise again as the doctor bent over her, to adjust the tubing. "You b–!" he cursed, as she vomited into the crook of his elbow.

It was the last straw. Everyone had had enough. The tube was withdrawn with a violent swiftness. Emily felt as though her throat had been stroked with a saw.

She vomited a third time, and then passed out. She came round to an empty cell and the slow realisation that the feeding was over and the party dispersed. She moaned softly and twisted her head this way and that on sheets which were wet with sick and sweat. Her hair was covered in vomit. Her mouth was bloody, but ungagged. From the cell next door came a tapping on the wall. It was Morse Code, as adapted by the Militant Suffragettes. NO SURRENDER, spelt the taps. Emily Davison clenched her fist and answered back the same.

**

Emily was fed twelve times in the course of the next four days. After each feed she would lie on her back on her bed, moaning softly as the tears trickled into her ears. But she never lay still for long at a time, always forcing herself to stand up and pace the small confines of her cell. For she was determined to keep as fit as she could, in preparation for whatever work awaited her outside.

Not that she was able to fix her mind on the world. The worst thing about prison, she decided, more awful even than the feeding, was the impossibility of forgetting that you were there. Most of the time Emily's thoughts circled, like seagulls, around the image of herself strapped to her bed, with the doctor leaning over and the tube going in. Should she just lie back and let the feeding happen? The pain would be less, she knew, but what was the point of refusing food in the first place if you weren't going to resist forcible feeding in the second?

***

"CLEAR THE DOOR! THIS IS AN ORDER! REMOVE ALL OBSTRUCTION!"

No response.

"Remove the barricade at once Davison. AT ONCE D'YOU HEAR ME!?"

Emily sat tight. She'd heard alright.

The idea for the barricade had come to her in a flash on the fifth day after the feeding began. She'd been moved to another cell which had two narrow single beds instead of the regulation one. It had been the work of an hour to change the furniture around, and line up both beds between the door and the opposite wall. They had fitted with pleasing exactness. Then Emily had piled the table and mattresses on top of the beds before cowering underneath her makeshift camp and waiting for the hated trolley to creak to a halt outside her door.

"Remove the barricade. Davison, I order you now to remove the barricade!"

"Open now and you shan't be punished. Any more and you'll… "

It was difficult for the authorities to think of what to threaten her with. She was already starving, already in solitary, already being tortured. What more could they do?

They were afraid of forcing open the door in case it fell inward onto the prisoner. The last thing the authorities wanted was a death on their hands. It was the visiting magistrate who fixed on the flooding plan: "Davison, if you don't open the door now we shall turn the hosepipe on you."

No answer.

The appearance of a ladder at the window – which looked onto the courtyard below – was closely followed by the smash and tinkle of broken glass. Emily just had time to look up and clock the nozzle of the hosepipe before the water hit her in an icy rush. It hit her and carried on hitting her, in stinging spurts which left her gasping for breath.

She closed her eyes against the horror and tried to turn what was happening to her body into something else in her head. She began by imagining herself on the last exhausting leg of a marathon swim.

Another gush. Another fit of violent shivers. It wasn't any good – it was what it was and it was hell and nothing like a bathe even in the roughest sea.

For ten long minutes the water careered onto the suffragette wedged between the beds. The cell became first a puddle, and then a pool. Emily began to shake uncontrollably. Then she heard, through the clatter of her chattering teeth, the words which spelt the end of the ordeal.

"Stop! That's enough. Turn it off."

It was the Doctor's voice. He'd heard, in a pause between the spurts of water, spasms in the suffragette's breathing which suggested that she might be about to pass out.

Once again the authorities commanded the suffragette to open the door. Once again the suffragette responded by not responding.

"Force the door." It was the Doctor speaking, again. "Watch out Davison! You might get hurt!" Emily smiled to hear the panic in his voice.

"You are more afraid of killing me than I am of dying," were the words she had in her head to say but neither her tongue nor her lips would do as they were told. Only her teeth moved, up and down, like castanets.

The door began to give. Emily sat very still, watching and waiting and wondering if this was the end and what the end was and what would happen to the movement after the end.

Would a death force the government to reconsider?

Would one dead woman mean votes for all the rest?

The door was opening, falling inwards. Four hairy

fingers appeared on either side, clutching it as it fell, stopping it from falling further.

A warder squeezed through into the cell as the water flooded the corridor.

Emily felt his hot angry breath in her face as he pulled her to her feet by her hair.

"You ought to be horsewhipped for this!" he shouted, shaking her.

But he couldn't shake her more than she was already shaking. Nor could he stop her spirit from soaring.

TOEING THE LINE

Mrs Davison was grim-faced as she nursed her frail daughter back to health over Christmas.

"Why does she look so old and ill?" asked Emily's married sister, who lived in France and hadn't seen Emily for about five years.

Mrs Davison, silenced by tears she would not shed, gave no answer.

"It's so odd," persisted the sister, who, though bored by ideas, was obsessed by appearances, "her teeth look as though they don't fit any more."

"Probably because they don't," said Mrs Davison, recovering herself. "She bought some false ones on special offer after a couple of hers were knocked out by the feeding… They're men's teeth really."

"Ugggh!" said the sister. "How dis-gus-ting!"

That was that as far as Emily's sister was concerned. From that moment on, whenever she heard mention of women's rights, she would think about men's teeth.

Mrs Davison, older, wiser, sadder, thought deeper. She wasn't fussed that Emily had lost her looks, but heartbroken to think that she had lost her mind.

***

Not everyone saw it like that of course. The hosepipe incident made Emily, briefly, something of a heroine at headquarters. Christabel wrote her a personal letter of praise and congratulation, and included with this the offer of a salaried post as official organiser for the Women's Social and Political Union.

"What's that then?" asked her mother, frowning.

"It's the name of the organisation that I belong to," explained Emily happily. "The one set up by the Pankhursts."

Mrs Davison nodded. "Not much to live on," she said, reading the terms and conditions over her daughter's shoulder.

Emily said nothing. The hunger strike wasn't her only reason for looking thin. The salary – at £2 a week – was rather more than she had become used to.

She returned to London to find an atmosphere of quiet elation at headquarters. The Liberals had taken a hammering at the general election of January 1910. They were in government still, but only just, and the Prime Minister had at last agreed to the formation of an all-party committee to look into the subject of women's suffrage. The women at the Union had responded, gratefully, with a suspension of their militant activities.

The result, for Emily, was a period of relative quiet during which she concentrated on the peaceful aspects of the campaign such as writing letters, raising funds and making speeches. She also wrote a series of articles for the suffragette newspaper, *Votes for Women* about women who had, in the past, made a difference by being different. She spent long hours in the British library, reading and writing and sometimes dreaming. She imagined future generations of women sitting where she was sitting, reading about the struggle for the vote and maybe... just maybe... about the part played in that struggle by... No. It didn't bear thinking about. Back to business. Back to work. Back to the life and times of Florence Nightingale.

In the spring of 1910 the all-party committee published the Conciliation Bill. This Bill, if made into law, would give the vote to a small number of women with money of their own. The Union was not the only organisation in England at that time campaigning for women's rights. There were several other, non-militant suffrage societies – which, between them, had many more members than the Pankhurst organisation – and they at once threw their weight behind the new Bill. For a week or two the arguments raged at Union headquarters about whether or not the militants should follow suit.

"It's too narrow," said some. "It's for widows and spinsters only; it does nothing for the working woman."

"It's a beginning." Christabel answered. "A foot in the door. Half a loaf is better than none," she added, as though that clinched the matter.

Which it did, in a way. For just as the rank and file looked to Mrs Pankhurst for leadership, Mrs

Pankhurst looked to her eldest daughter. "Unity is everything," said the older woman, with a hint of apology, as she climbed off the fence and went into the Conciliation camp. "And Christabel's word is law," muttered the malcontents, under their breath. The arguments subsided, and the truce continued.

"How much do you like Christabel, really?" Mary asked Emily once, over a cup of cocoa in their favourite Lyons corner shop just round the corner from headquarters.

"I think she's… " Emily began then stopped, blushing. Mrs Tuke was standing by the counter, waiting to pay for a bag of buns and a packet of biscuits.

"I think you agree with me," said Mary, quietly, watching the Poodle's back. "You think she's autocratic and overbearing. But we don't dare say so, do we, because unity is everything and who are we to disagree?"

***

Emily's night in the House of Commons heating cupboard was completely unplanned. She'd intended only getting as far as the lobby, from where she'd send a message to the Prime Minister. He wouldn't reply, of course. He never did. But she would at least have reminded him that the militant spirit lived on, truce or no truce.

It was only once she was inside the building that it occurred to her that she might do something a little more daring. She'd darted into a corridor marked private and then, hearing footsteps, climbed through a window set into the wall and found herself among a mass of ladders and pipes. She had stumbled upon the heating apparatus of the House, she realised with a start, and wedged herself in.

What followed was the least comfortable night of Emily's life. She spent much of it thinking over some of the things which were being said among militants, about Union policy. Mary was not the only one who was critical of Christabel's leadership. Emily had several other disaffected friends, who all complained of the same thing: the feeling that their opinions didn't count with Christabel, that they were valued only as foot soldiers. "Let-democracy-begin; At-Clement's-Inn!" was one of the rebellious chants, doing secret rounds.

The talk reminded Emily of the angry muttering in

the staffroom of a school where she had briefly worked, in between governessing jobs. She hadn't liked it then and she didn't like it now. Emily was a loner by nature but not by choice: the sense of collective enthusiasm for the Cause had been one of the things which had most attracted her, in the beginning, about the Union. But disunity frightened her – throughout her life, whenever rival gangs had begun to form, her impulse had been to run away and read a book.

Not that she did much reading now. More because she couldn't concentrate than because she hadn't time. "I see the vote as a latchkey," Mary Leigh had said to her once. "It may be a little thing in itself, but women need to have that little thing in their possession before they can build any sort of independence."

It was a key to the past as well as the future, Emily thought now: only after the vote was won would she have her mind to herself again, free to wander wherever books led. For the time being she was in mental as well as physical limbo: wedged between hot pipes in the House of Commons heating cupboard, thinking only of the stir her presence would create, when she was found. "They're everywhere, damned women! Absolutely everywhere!" – who had said that, and when? she wondered, sleepily, as she fell at last into a fitful doze.

She was discovered, hours later, by the night watchman. He nearly dropped his lantern in surprise and no wonder: her face, neck and hands were black with grime and this combined with the green of her eyes and the tangled dusty redness of her hair to suggest a wild thing from another, unknown world.

At the police station they asked her, again and again how she had done it but all they ever got in answer was a maddening shake of her small narrow head and a secretive knowing smile. After two hours she was released on the special orders of the Home Secretary who thought the government could do without the publicity a trial would entail. The newspapers ran the story all the same and Emily, proud of her adventure, was surprised to receive nothing in the way of a note or card from headquarters.

Surprised but undisturbed: everyone was very busy suddenly, working flat out for a huge procession which had been planned for June. It was possible that Christabel had missed the newspaper report.

The Conciliation Bill, meanwhile, had been passed by the House of Commons. Success at last! All that was needed now was for the government to agree to give parliamentary time for the details to be worked out. The June procession, which had been planned as a peaceful demonstration, turned into a triumphal march.

Emily was proud to take her place in the Prisoners' Pageant, along with more than six hundred other women who had gone to prison for the Cause. They all wore white, with prison medals – distributed by the Union – pinned to their chests. In their hands they carried standards, topped by a broad arrow – the emblem of their imprisonment. Except for the four women at the very front: they were busy holding up a large banner, on which the words "From Prison to Citizenship" were emblazoned in a loud splash of purple, white and green.

More than ten thousand women altogether marched along the Embankment in the blazing sunshine. Most were far from being militant – many indeed had been actively opposed to the suffragettes' breaking of the law – but they all supported votes for women. Some were recent converts, others life-long believers. But no one who took part in that procession ever forgot the peculiar atmosphere of happy hopefulness which coloured the day.

**

It didn't last. What had the women been thinking of? When the Prime Minister was asked, in the House of Commons, for a date on which the details of the Conciliation Bill could be further debated, he pleaded pressure of more important business and refused to answer.

Emily's hopes for the Bill evaporated as she read the evening paper. She was all alone at the time, sitting in the Lyons corner shop, and the rage burst out of her.

"The scoundrel!" she shouted, waving her newspaper in the air. "The Prime Minister is a wicked liar!"

A waitress came with the bill at once. The proprietor didn't want a scene.

The suffragette paid up in a daze. The Prime Minister had made clear his contempt for the suffragettes, so she, Emily Wilding Davison, would make clear hers for him. Who cared if her return to militancy only further antagonised the authorities? The suffragettes had been peaceful as pie for months, and where had that got them?

Emily left the tea shop and walked towards White-hall, where all the government offices were. About halfway there she stopped at a building site, and slipped under the makeshift fence to fetch a smallish brick for her largish handbag. Then she hurried on.

She went for the first building she recognised: it was the crown office and it had a large sash window, on the ground floor, looking onto the street, begging to be smashed. Emily looked around, and saw two police constables just the right distance away. Not close enough to stop her doing what she was about to do, but not far enough for her to make the escape she didn't want to make.

One, two, three, crasharoony! The brick was heavier than the stones she was used to throwing and the whole pane shattered inwards, making the most tremendous racket. The constables came running and took her roughly by the arms.

"Best place for you is behind bars," said one of the policemen, frogmarching her down to the station.

"I agree," said Emily Davison, smiling serenely.

The leadership didn't. Emily Davison's fine was paid without her knowledge or permission.

She felt a fool, walking free from court when she'd braced herself for a spell in jail. There was a terse letter waiting for her at her lodgings. It was from Christabel, demanding that she call in at Clement's Inn as soon as possible. Emily went at once.

She found Mrs Tuke alone, writing letters, trying to raise money for the cause.

"Why was my fine paid?" asked Emily, sounding cross.

"Policy," said Mrs Tuke, looking unhappy. "The truce."

"I see," said Emily, feeling stupid.

"Is Christabel angry with me?" asked Emily then. She felt something was wrong, but couldn't tell what.

"No," said the poodle, "She's not angry. It's just…"

Mrs Tuke could not finish her sentence: Christabel was standing in the door.

"Thank you for coming in, Miss Davison," said Christabel, motioning her to sit down before sliding into her own chair behind her desk.

"You asked to see me."

"Of course I did," said Christabel, drumming her fingers together as though she couldn't for the life of her remember the reason why.

"I... I smuggled into the House of Commons," said Emily, then, to break the awkward silence. "I spent a night in the heating cupboard."

"Yes," said Christabel. "We heard."

"I nearly died of thirst," Emily was babbling now, but couldn't stop, "and the watchman who found me nearly died of fright."

"Yes," said Christabel. "Yes, I'm sure."

"It got a mention in the *The Times*. Did you see?"

"Yes," said Christabel. "Yes, I read the report."

Pause.

"Was there something wrong with my action?" asked Emily at length, feeling the question forced out of her.

"Well," said Christabel, "you know our rule is to have no rules. Women are free to make whatever protest they see fit against a government which not see reason."

"Exactly," said Emily. "That's what I thought.

That's why I didn't think to tell… "

"But the case, as you should know, is slightly different at the moment," Christabel interrupted. "There is a truce."

"I thought," said Emily, "that the truce just covered official protests."

"It covers officials full stop. You, Miss Davison, are a salaried worker for this organisation. The newspapers describe you as such when writing up your escapades. It looks as though we can't control you. It is a problem."

"I'm sorry," said Emily. She wasn't really. She was furious. The truce, in her view, had manifestly failed. Why should she toe the line?

"Don't be sorry," said Christabel. "Be straight. You don't believe in the truce. Why should you toe the line?"

Emily looked down, embarrassed. She'd forgotten Christabel's talent for reading minds.

"Miss Davison – may I call you Emily, please?"

Emily nodded, blushing with pleasure. It was a sign of friendship, surely, that Christabel wanted to call her by her Christian name?

"You, Emily, are a free spirit. That is your great strength."

Emily basked in the unfamiliar praise. She wasn't in trouble after all. Relief flooded through her.

"I don't want to clip your wings, Emily. I admire your initiative."

Another pause. The word initiative hung, accusingly, in the air.

Emily knew that she had to show some of what was being praised. And fast.

"Would it be better if I became a freelance militant?" she asked. "If I gave up my official position?"

"What a good idea," said Christabel, as though the solution had only at that moment occurred to her. "Then you could keep your independence."

The deed was done – signed, sealed and settled – within minutes of being suggested. Emily left the office a few minutes later, after thanking Christabel for her kindness in making her jobless.

As she clattered down the stone staircase she remembered her first visit to the office, five years earlier. At that time she had been alarmed by the aggressive tactics pioneered by the Union; now she was frustrated by its peaceful politicking.

"The Movement's changed," she thought. "But so have I."

DEEPER AND DEEPER

"Excuse me, Miss." Emily Davison jumped at the familiar tap on the shoulder. She was standing in front of a pillar box. In her hand was a rag soaked in paraffin. In her bag was a box of household matches. On her face was an expression of gleeful guilt.

"Good afternoon officer," Emily said. "Is this what we call a red-handed catch?"

The policeman shook his head. He couldn't believe these women. They looked like ladies and acted like layabouts. This one, unless he was very much mistaken, had been about to set fire to the contents of the pillar box.

"Are you going to arrest me?" asked Emily then. "I

think you'd better. It would have been my third fire today."

The policeman sighed and did as he was told. Why, he wondered, as he escorted Emily down to the station, would anyone see burning other folks' letters as a reason for giving women the vote?

"It's all about the value of nuisance," said Emily, doing a Christabel, reading his mind.

The trial was held over until the New Year when Emily Davison stood in the dock and declared that the pillar box fires had been her own idea entirely. She was sentenced to six months. Old Mrs Davison, who had come up to London especially, sat at the back and wept as her daughter was carted off to Holloway to begin her sixth prison sentence.

Mrs Davison went on by foot to the offices of the Women's Social and Political Union. It was her first visit to London for many years and she was wide-eyed at the changes. In Northumberland the motor car was still a rarity but here there were more motor-taxis than there were horse-drawn hansoms. Mrs Davison had an inkling that the motor would make more difference to voters than the vote ever would to women.

"I've come to talk to you about my daughter," she announced to no one in particular, as she stood in the open doorway of the office, puffing from the stairs.

Mrs Tuke looked up. She was used to parents' visits. Usually the fathers came, shouting abuse and making empty threats.

"Please come in," she said, "your daughter is...?"

"In prison. Six months."

"I'm sorry. I'm not sure… "

"Well I am. Poor lamb doesn't know what she's talking about. 'I did the the fires on my own,' she tells the court. Well they might not know better, but I do. I don't know your name but I know your shame. You got my girl involved and now you've dropped her and now she's worse than ever."

"Are you Emily's mother?" asked Mrs Tuke, with a sinking feeling.

"No actually. I'm the Queen of England," said Mrs Davison, sitting down at last and folding her arms across her chest.

Poodle Tuke took a deep breath. She'd always wondered where Emily had got her spirit from.

"The trouble with Emily is… " she began.

"The trouble with Emily is the trouble she's in... and who got her in it, that's what I'd like to know!"

"What exactly would you like us to do?" asked Mrs Tuke evenly.

"I'd like you to look after my daughter when she comes out of prison. Find her a job which doesn't involve spells inside. Otherwise she'll die. Her health's not up to it."

There was a silence during which Christabel opened the door from the inner office and stood there, forbiddingly. Mrs Tuke made the introductions. Mrs Davison continued to sit.

"I hate asking you this," she said, not looking at either woman now. "I don't like your attitudes and I don't agree with your politics. But Emily doesn't listen to me anymore. She never listened to me much but she stopped altogether a few years back, when she first got involved with you."

Christabel spoke first. "Your daughter is no use to us, Mrs Davison. She cannot obey orders."

Mrs Davison bridled. "But that's what your movement is all about, isn't it? Obedient girls don't throw stones in the first place."

"You'd be surprised," answered Christabel, coldly smiling as she pulled shut the connecting door.

***

For a while Emily was the only suffragette in her prison wing. Then a great batch of militants arrived together with news of the world outside. The truce was finally over – not because the government had given in but because it hadn't. Mrs. Pankhurst had announced that "the argument of the stone" was now the only one left to them. Whole streets of windows had been smashed during one carefully orchestrated evening promenade.

Mrs Pankhurst herself had been sentenced to nine months and was expected to join the rest of them in Holloway. Christabel, who had also been arrested, had escaped to France. She was living in Paris under a false name, directing operations by post and courier.

"What sort of daughter is it that lets her old mother bear the brunt?" asked one of the wardresses, trying to get the suffragettes to talk. But Emily and her friends, refusing to play, kept up a smiling silence. Christabel was a tyrant; her mother was a saint. The suffragettes knew, or thought they knew, that the Movement needed both.

***

"Pssst. She's here."

"Where?"

"Next floor down."

"She got privileges?"

"Course."

"Why?"

"They didn't want to risk her going on the hunger strike, that's why."

"They didn't want to risk feeding her, more like."

"They wouldn't dare, anyway."

"Whatever. We know what we've got to do now."

"S'pose."

"You on, Emily?"

"Of course I am."

It had already been arranged, on the outside, that the suffragettes would hunger strike if their leader were treated any differently from themselves. The authorities weren't going to be allowed to rule by dividing. If Mrs Pankhurst was a political prisoner, who deserved to be treated better than a common criminal, then so too were they.

Emily joined in the protest with a heavy heart. It was the feeding she dreaded, rather than the starving. The trolley rounds began two days into the strike. Emily sat in her cell, listening to the protesting cries of the other prisoners, praying for deliverance.

**

"What the… "

"Stop her! Stop her before she jumps!"

"How did she…?"

"Too late now. There ain't no stopping that one!"

"She's one of the worst, isn't she?"

"Well I don't know about that. She's been quiet enough these past few months."

The voices of her gaolers drifted up to Emily as she stood at the top of the iron staircase which ran across the centre of the building in which most of the suffragettes were being held. She felt floaty with hunger and sick with fear.

"Davison!"

"Davison come down at once!"

"Don't be a fool woman!"

"If you jump from there you'll crack your skull!"

"Do you actually want to die?"

But Emily only knew what she didn't want. She didn't want to have a steel gag forced into her mouth and a tube down her throat. She didn't want to listen to the screams of other prisoners resisting the feeders as she waited for her turn to come. She didn't want this agony to go on and on and on, with never a change or a result...

"No surrender!" shouted one of the prisoners, watching from the corridor below.

"No surrender!" echoed Emily, and blindly jumped.

***

"Darling," said Mrs Davison, sitting on the edge of her daughter's bed and speaking with unaccustomed gentleness. "You're not well."

Emily closed her eyes. Of course she wasn't well. That wasn't the point was it? The point was to *force* the government to give women the vote. To see justice done. To show the Prime Minister that the suffragettes were not to be trifled with. To show Christabel that... ouch, ouch, ouch if only her head didn't ache so. Even when she was lying down she felt as though she were thinking from inside an engine room.

"You could have killed yourself," said Mrs Davison, not for the first time.

"I wish I had," thought Emily, not for the last.

Would a suffragette death bring the government to its senses? It was common knowledge that Mrs Pankhurst was quite prepared to lay down her life for the Cause. That was why the authorities did not dare to feed the leader by force. They were afraid of the strength of her resistance. They were afraid that if they began by feeding her they would end by killing her. They were afraid of the power of martyrdom.

"Your leader's been arrested again," said Mrs Davison the next day. "I heard it in the shop. They say she's taken responsibility for the fires which have been breaking out in empty buildings."

Emily said nothing.

"Tell me it's not true, darling. Tell me it's not your friends starting these fires."

Emily pretended not to hear. Past were the days when she begged her mother to let her explain. Past too were the days when Mrs Davison refused to listen. Now it was all the other way round. Tell me this, promise me that, explain the other, her mother would say. And Emily wouldn't. Not because she didn't want to but because she didn't dare. After the ending of the truce, the movement had become more militant than ever before and the police more vigilant. The best protection for loved ones was ignorance.

"Answer me when I speak to you Emily Davison."

"Mother, please!"

"Has your leader authorised arson?"

"Why would she not?" asked Emily, cornered. "You know our policy. And the buildings are always empty," she added, on a pleading note.

"You can never be sure of that!"

"Well… "

"Don't you 'well' me, you wicked child."

Emily, startled, left the house and went for a walk on the moor. Were the fires so much worse than what had gone before? In her heart the daughter knew that her mother was, if not right, then at least not completely wrong. Arson was playing with fire in more ways than one. But… but… but… Would arson work where first peaceful protest and then acts of minor sabotage had failed? The militants no longer thought in terms of persuading the politicians to see reason: it was now a question of forcing politicians who couldn't care less to do the right thing for the sake of a quiet life.

**

After two hours on the moor Emily returned home to find her mother hunched in her rocking chair, looking utterly broken.

"You don't trust me," said the old woman, staring at her daughter.

"Oh mother!" cried Emily, crouching down beside her. And then she told her mother everything she knew about the new law which had been passed by the government. Suffragettes released early because of illness could now be rearrested at any time. The Cat and Mouse Act – so-called by the women because of the way the larger creature plays with the smaller, pretending to give it back its freedom, then pouncing again just when it is about to reach a place of safety – was the reason for the new culture of secrecy.

"We don't look for arrest any more. We need to be free... but many of the women have had to go into hiding for fear of rearrest. They call themselves mice... I may have to join them, Mother. If you don't hear from me for a while that will be the reason why. The others won't know... Nobody knows for sure what anyone else is doing any more, Mother. It's safer that way, don't you see?"

Mrs Davison only saw that her daughter was in deeper than ever. The vote, she noticed, which once she'd longed for as the only possible cure for her daughter's madness, was no longer mentioned.

"The fight has swallowed the goal," thought the old woman, sadly.

GALLOPING HOOVES

In London Emily house-sat for friends of the movement who had gone away for the summer, leaving her a larder full of food and a welcome stash of petty cash. She began work planning a lecture which she had been asked to give to the Workers' Education Association. "A chain is only as strong as its weakest link," she wrote, underlining the last two words, "and women are the weakest link in the economic chain."

Lots of men were afraid that, if women had the vote, the rates of pay for working women would improve and the pay packets of working men would suffer accordingly. Emily hoped to persuade her audience that if the position of working women were improved then the labour movement as a whole would be strenghtened.

"But what's the point really?" she exclaimed, after an afternoon spent hunched over her notes. "It's the government, not the working man, that we need to convince." And then she put her notes away, and began thinking about her next protest.

Mary Leigh turned up in the middle of the night. She looked a wreck. She'd been in Dublin, where she'd been sentenced to five years penal servitude after first throwing a hatchet into the Prime Minister's carriage and then setting fire to an empty box at the Theatre Royal. She had gone on hunger strike of course, and been forcibly fed, and then she'd been questioned for hours at a time by a visiting psychiatrist.

"Why?" asked Emily, knowing the answer, dreading to hear it.

"They wanted to have me certified. To lock me up as a lunatic. Out of harm's way."

Emily shivered. Everyone knew it was a one-way street into the asylum. Once certified the women could be put away for years at a time and no one on the outside would be able to do a thing about it.

"The good news is they didn't succeed," croaked Mary, seeing Emily's stricken face. Mary had been released on licence after several weeks of forced feeding. "So now I'm just another mouse in hiding," she explained, climbing into Emily's bed.

***

Mary went away again the next day and Emily felt a wave of desolation wash over her. "You are a free spirit," Christabel had said.

Emily was not so sure. She longed for the sense of happy comradeship with other women which had buoyed her up in the early days of militancy. She was an outsider now, partly by her own choice, partly by Christabel's command, and she regretted it daily. She hadn't much liked obeying orders, it was true; but that was nothing to the loneliness of not receiving any.

For the first time since becoming a suffragette Emily was afraid of the future. She was afraid that the next time the doctors tried to feed her by force that the food would enter her lungs, and she would die.

"And that," said Emily out loud, as she took a long calm look at her haggard face in the bedroom mirror, "would be a waste of a life."

She lay down on the bed and fixed her mind, once more, on the details of her next protest. The important thing was not to botch it. To go out with a bang. No more staircase falls behind prison walls. It took a spectacle to make a splash.

***

Derby Day, 1913. Emily Davison half-stepped, half-fell on to the station platform, where she was at once pushed forward and held back by the mass of other passengers all around her. It was a happy atmosphere, squish-squash, but not criss-cross. Faces were smiling and voices were laughing and short legs weaving in and out of longer ones. Parents were relaxed about letting their children forge ahead, content in the knowledge that everyone was part of a crowd headed in the same direction: out of the station up the hill towards the racecourse.

Early that morning Emily had gone to the headquarters and heard the news. Mrs Pankhurst had been released again, after refusing drink as well as food.

"She's very ill," said Mrs Tuke, with tears in her eyes. "But they'll rearrest her as soon as she gets up from her sickbed. She won't give up, that's the trouble. She'd rather die first."

Mrs Pankhurst was the "Queen of the Mice". While Christabel remained in Paris, her mother had been in and out of prison like a yoyo. She had a three-year sentence hanging over her for an arson attack on an empty house belonging to the Chancellor. Everyone knew she hadn't been anywhere near the property at the time but that wasn't the point. The point was that she had taken full responsibilty.

Emily hadn't liked to linger at the office. The atmosphere there had changed from one of fervour to one of fear since the arson campaign began. A recent police raid had resulted in the arrest of all the office staff on the premises at the time.

It was said that Christabel was losing her grip. Recently a few of the old guard had gone to Paris to suggest a change of direction. Let the doubters and sceptics go their own way, Christabel had replied, tightening her grip.

Emily couldn't bear the thought of the movement to which she'd given her life collapsing in divisions and squabbles. It wouldn't happen, she thought, as long as

Mrs Pankhurst was around to hold it together. Christabel was dangerous. Her mother was indispensible.

"I want two flags," said Emily, the morning of the Derby.

"What are they for?" Mrs Tuke asked, without much interest, as she fished the scraps of purple, white and green out of a box.

It was only later, when she heard the news, that she recalled Emily's silence, and the funny half-smile which had accompanied it, and then she wailed with grief and guilt about the sadness and the waste.

***

"You coming or going, miss, 'cos some of us is tired of waitin'."

Emily was in a dream, holding up the queue. She apologised quickly and moved forward, handing in her ticket at the barrier, before dashing off towards the train.

"Oi miss, don't you need your return?" called the inspector.

"Thank you," said Emily, blushing and taking back the ticket. A special Derby day offer from

Victoria station had made a return cheaper than a single. Would she need it? Hard to say.

Emily, trying to melt into the crowd, felt a hot discomfort in her badly chosen clothes. All the other women, she noticed now, wore brightly coloured silks and carried parasols and lightly woven shawls over their arms. Emily, by contrast, was in a long woollen coat buttoned up tight to her neck. She longed to take it off, but what would she do then with the flags secreted inside? There was nothing for it but to sweat it out and pray to God that no one would suspect her reason for looking different.

It wouldn't do for anyone to guess that here was a dangerous criminal, recently released from a spell in prison, liable to reoffend at any time.

**

"Psst Emily, over here!"

Emily had been going in the direction of Tattenham Corner, one of the most popular vantage points for the race. Hearing her name she stopped walking and turned round to see a young, boyish-looking woman standing on a bank just above her.

Emily recognised her as a recent recruit. What

was her name? She couldn't remember.

"Here for a reason?"

"Yes. I… " Emily's voice faltered.

The young woman moved on with a wink and a smile. Emily stared after her, willing her to turn back. She felt very afraid, suddenly. Afraid and alone, despite the crowds milling about, pushing her forward.

But the nameless woman had seen the panic in Emily's eyes and she had no intention of turning back. She knew Emily Davison's reputation as one of the wildest of the older members of the Union and she did not doubt that whatever she'd intended to do was better done than not. DEEDS NOT WORDS was the motto of their movement. Spill the milk and be done with weeping.

***

Emily put a shaky foot forward and made a conscious effort to pull herself together. She breathed deeply, twice, and thought about the day when women would be free.

The race was due to begin. Funny time for time to fly, she thought, taking her position at Tattenham

Corner, close to the fence which separated the spectators from the riders.

Why her? Why now? Because she was alone in the world except for her mother, and her mother's heart was already broken. If she went now perhaps God, in His mercy, would spare Mrs Pankhurst. How many deaths would it take to make the Liberal Government see sense?

***

The race began with a bang. There were fifteen runners altogether. Emily strained her long neck to get a better view. Behind her a mass of spectators began to call out the names of whatever horse they had put their money on.

"Anmer" was the name most often called out. Anmer was the King's horse, the favourite, and Emily had an idea that he was the glossy chestnut slightly separated from the others, a few paces behind on the outside lane.

The noise of the crowd was deafening. Emily could smell her own fear. She undid two buttons around her chest and slipped a hand inside her coat. The race was no longer in sight – any minute now the horses would reappear around the corner and gallop past. She drew out one of the small union flags and held it as tight as she could in fingers slippery with sweat.

The horses were coming. Anmer had fallen a good few paces behind now. "Perfect!" thought Emily, seeing the fuss ahead. Much better the King's horse than any other. There was a rush of hooves as the leading dozen thundered past. "Now or never!" said Emily out loud, breaking into a run, waving her flag in their air.

Everyone who witnessed it never forgot what happened next. A tall, thin woman, with greying hair flying loose in the wind, standing on the racetrack, waving her arms in the direction of the three remaining oncoming horses.

Despairing shouts went up from the bank of seats at Tattenham Corner as the woman reached out to catch the bridle of the King's horse in her hand, and was knocked to the ground. Blood gushed from her mouth and nose. The horse, meanwhile, somersaulted backwards, kicking the woman on the way, one blow hitting her straight in the head. The woman rolled over, and lay spreadeagled on the ground, with empty eyes wide open on the crowd.

VOTES FOR WOMEN! read the flag which fluttered in the breeze.

"Vote for witches more like!" growled one of the emergency men involved in removing Emily Davison's body from the racecourse.

EPILOGUE

Emily Davison never again recovered consciousness. She died four days later, on June 8th 1913. The days were spent in Epsom College Hospital, close to the racecourse, where Mary Leigh was the first of a steady stream of friends who came to pay their last respects.

Christabel sent a telegram from Paris to the headquarters saying that no trouble or expense was to be spared in the planning of the funeral. The result was a suffragette demonstration which was remembered forever by the thousands who took part, and by the hundreds of thousands who lined the streets to watch the women go by.

The procession began at Victoria Station, where

Emily's body had arrived from Epsom.

First came the standard bearer, a beautiful young woman whose cropped hair and limpid features gave her the look of a medieval saint as she marched in front carrying a huge wooden cross. She was followed by a group of twelve girls dressed in white who carried laurel wreaths and a purple banner on which the words FIGHT ON and GOD WILL GIVE THE VICTORY were embroidered in silver. After the girls in white came a dense throng of women in black carrying bunches of purple irises, and after them a solemn stream of Union members, all dressed in white with tall Madonna lilies in their hands.

The horse-drawn hearse came next. The coffin was covered with a purple cloth, edged with silver, held in place by wreaths of flowers in the shape of prison arrows. Women in military dress marched by the coffin, and behind came all the recently arrested office staff, who were awaiting trial.

Their everyday clothes gave them the appearance of marked women amid the sea of uniform. Behind the office staff came the empty carriage which had been meant for Mrs Pankhurst – she had been arrested on her way to Victoria, just as soon as she had stepped outside in fact, and had ordered that her carriage appear in the procession without her, with darkened windows to indicate her absence.

"Upstaged even in death," murmured a malcontent, one of a group of marching drummers who brought up the rear of the procession.

The crowds in the street were awed and silent except for the odd raucous shout from boys making trouble.

"Three cheers for the King's jockey!" cried one.

"Whatever 'appened to the poor old 'orse?" answered back another.

The procession paused for a brief funeral service at St George's in Hart Street – the absent Christabel was the only person alive likely to know the significance of the venue – before going on to King's Cross, from where it had been arranged that the coffin would travel north, for a churchyard burial in the family plot.

***

Throughout this time Mrs Davison had remained at home where she was besieged by reporters. What was her daughter like, really? Where had she gone wrong?

"No comment," said the mother. "No, really... I've nothing to say."

Nor, after Emily's death, did she want anything to do with the splendid martyr's funeral being arranged for her daughter at the Union headquarters.

"More use to them dead than alive," was what she thought, bitterly, when she heard of the girls in white and the women in black, the flowers and the singing, the service at St George's, and the long funeral march.

When the body came home at last, by train from King's Cross, there were still crowds trailing the coffin.

"You must be so proud... " said strangers, holding out their hands to the old woman, stopping only when they saw the thunder in her face.

Mrs Davison wasn't proud. She never had been. "I want her back," was all she ever said on the subject of her daughter's death.

***

Women over 30 were given the vote in 1918, after the war. The rest had to wait until 1928.

Key Dates

1872 - Emily Davison born at Blackheath.

1878 - Women admitted for degrees at London University for the first time.

1891 - Emily starts studying for a degree at one of the new women's colleges attached to London University.

1893 - Emily's father dies. She leaves university and embarks on a teaching career.

1903 - The Women's Social and Political Union (WSPU) is founded by Mrs Pankhurst and her daughter Christabel.

1905 - Christabel Pankhurst and another woman are sent to prison after interrupting a political meeting. The Daily Mail calls them "suffragettes".

1906 - The Liberals win the General Election.
      Emily becomes a member of the WSPU.

1909 - The hunger strike is adopted by suffragette prisoners in protest at their treatment.
      Emily resigns from and volunteers for Danger Work.
      She interrupts the Chancellor at a meeting in

Limehouse and is sent to Holloway Gaol. She goes on hunger strike and is released early.

Emily, in prison again, goes on hunger strike and is forcibly fed. She barricades herself into her cell and is flooded by a hosepipe.

1910 - Emily becomes a salaried worker for the WSPU.

The WSPU declare a truce after the government promises an all-party committee to look into the question of votes for women.

Emily breaks the truce, spending a night hidden in a House of Commons heating cupboard.

The all-party committee publishes the Conciliation Bill, which would give the vote to a small number of financially independent women. Ten thousand women march through London in favour of the Bill.

Emily breaks the truce again, after the Prime minister has refused to name a date for the Bill to be debated.

Emily resigns from her salaried post.

1911 - Emily sets fire to a pillar box. She is sentenced to six months imprisonment.

1912 - The WSPU give up hope of justice from the government and declare the truce over. Mrs Pankhurst announces "the argument of the stone" is the only one left. Mass window-smashing in the West End. The suffragette leaders are arrested. Christabel escapes to France.

Emily throws herself from the prison staircase at Holloway, in protest at forcible feeding.

1913 - The Cat and Mouse Act, which allowed for the re-arrest of suffragette prisoners who had been released because of the hunger strike.

Mrs Pankhurst is sentenced to three years in prison after claiming responsibility for a fire-bomb.

Emily grabs the bridle of the King's Horse at the Derby. She died four days later.

Claudia FitzHerbert was born in 1965. She reviews regularly for the Daily Telegraph. She lives in Oxford with her children.

WHO WAS... Alexander Selkirk
Survivor on a Desert Island
Amanda Mitchison
1-904095-79-8

On the beach stood a wild thing waving its arms and hollering. The thing had the shape of a man, but it was all covered in fur, like a Barbary ape. What was it? A new kind of animal? A monster?

It was Alexander Selkirk, Scottish mariner and adventurer, thrilled to be rescued by passing sailors after four years alone on a Pacific island. This is the story of how Selkirk came to be stranded on the island and how he survived, the story of...
THE REAL ROBINSON CRUSOE.

WHO WAS... Ada Lovelace
Computer Wizard of Victorian England
Lucy Lethbridge
1-904095-76-3

Daughter of the famous poet Lord Byron, Ada
Lovelace was a child prodigy. Brilliant at maths, she
read numbers like most people read words.

In 1834 she came to the attention of Charles Babbage,
a scientist and techno0whizz who had just built an
amazing new 'THINKING MACHINE'. Ada and Mr
Babbage made a perfect partnership, which produced
the most important invention of the modern world –
THE COMPUTER!

WINNER OF THE BLUE PETER
BOOK AWARD 2002!

WHO WAS... David Livingstone
The Legendary Explorer
Amanda Mitchison
1-904095-84-4

Born a poor Glasgow cotton-mill worker, David grew up to become a great explorer and hero of his time.

This is his incredible story. The tough man of Victorian Britain would stop at nothing in his determination to be the first white man to explore Afirca, even if it meant dragging his wife and children along with him.

He trekked hundreds of miles through dangerous territory, braving terrible illness and pain, and was attacked by cannibals, rampaging lions and killer ants...

WHO WAS... Ned Kelly
Gangster Hero of the Australian Outback
Charlie Boxer
1-904095-61-5

Born into a family of Irish settlers in Australia, Ned
Kelly grew up bad. Cattle and horse thieving led him
into regular dust-ups with the law. Then, at 23, while
on the run, he shot a policeman dead.

For two years Ned and his gang of outlaws hid in the
outback, making a mockery of all attempts to catch
them. This is the story of how a bushranger declared
war on his country's police and became a great
national hero.

WHO WAS... Charlotte Bronte
The Girl Who Turned her Life into a Book
Kate Hubbard
1-904095-80-1

Of the famous Bronte siblings, Charlotte, the eldest, was the survivor. At eight, she was packed off to a boarding school so harsh that it killed two of her sisters. Her adult years were equally haunted by tragedy.

But one thing kept Charlotte going: she had a secret talent for story-telling. This is the tale of a remarkable woman, who turned her own life into one of the world's greatest classic novels, *Jane Eyre*.

WHO WAS... Anne Boleyn
The Queen Who Lost her Head
Laura Beatty
1-904095-78-X

For Anne Boleyn, King Henry VIII threw away his wife, out-raged his people, chucked his religion, and drove his best friend to death.

What does it take to drive a King this crazy? Was she a witch? An enchantress? Whatever she was, Anne turned Tudor England upside-down and shook it. And everyone was talking about her...

But Anne lived dangerously. And when she could not give the King the one thing he wanted – a son – his love went out like a light. The consequences for Anne were deadly...